superstars! superstars! superstars!

CREATIVE EDUCATION SPORTS SUPERSTARS

chuck
foreman

chuck
foreman

chuck foreman

by John deRosier

photographs by Carl Skalak, Jr.

CREATIVE EDUCATION
CHILDRENS PRESS

To my son, Tom, a sweet young man of seven years from his father - who loves him John deRosier

chuck foreman

Published by Creative Educational Society, Inc., 123 South Broad Street, Mankato, Minnesota 56001. Printed in the United States.

Library of Congress Cataloging in Publication Data
De Rosier, John.
Chuck Foreman.
SUMMARY: A brief biography of the star running back of the Minnesota Vikings football team.
1. Foreman, Chuck, 1950- —Juvenile literature.
2. Football players—United States—Biography—Juvenile literature.
[1. Foreman, Chuck, 1950- 2. Football players] I. Title.
GV939.F67D47 796.33'2'0924 [B] [92] 76-49561
ISBN 0-87191-543-X

chuck foreman

chuck foreman

It was a bright crisp day in Washington on November 30. It was to be a day of decision for the Washington Redskins. They had lost three recent games in overtime and if they lost again, they were probably out of the playoffs.

Their coach, George Allen, was a master at the psychological moves necessary to get a team up to win the big games. When the Redskins came out on the field they were "fired up."

The other team was the undefeated Vikings of Minnesota. The previous Thursday they had won the Central Division title for the seventh time in the last eight years. They were a great team, with all-pro players on offensive and defensive lines, at middle-linebacker, safety, quarterback, wide receiver, and running back. The all-pro at running back was a man who believed in "never giving up." His name was Chuck Foreman.

As soon as the game started, it was obvious that the Vikings were flat—too many titles won too soon. But the Redskins didn't have any title guaranteed and they were hungry. The Redskins were going to have the Vikings for breakfast.

For at least two quarters they did. Close to the end of the first half the score was Redskins 21, Vikings 0. With the aging Billy Kilmer directing the attack, the Skins went on drives of 67, 92 and 28 yards for their early lead. But the Vikings weren't dead; they had just been a little slow waking up that Sunday.

The Vikings go into their two minute drill as the first half ends. First, a 14-yard bolt up the middle by running back Ed Marinaro to the Washington three. First and ten. Quarterback Fran Tarkenton rolls right, throws to wide-receiver John Gilliam for touchdown. The official calls pass interference against the Vikings. No touchdown. First and ten, but this time on the 13-yard line; 24 seconds to go.

Fran Tarkenton calls two consecutive plays into the line. Neither one gains an inch against the fired-up Redskin defense. But the officials detect Redskin Pat Fisher holding Gilliam, five yard penalty. Third and five, this time on the eight yard line; nine seconds. Fran comes up to the line of scrimmage, bends to make the call, studies the defense, gets the ball, rolls out, looks to the primary receiver, Gilliam—covered; then to Chuck Foreman—covered, then to Marinaro—covered, back to Foreman, who has now shaken off his coverage, at the goal line. Fran throws, Chuck catches it. They score! At the end of the first half, the Vikings go into the locker room down 21-7.

As the second half begins it is obvious that now the Vikings are charged up. After the Redskins kick off, the Vikings go 71 yards in 13 plays to make the score 21-14. On the last play of that drive Chuck Foreman dives over from the one for the score. Washington comes right back with a Mike Bragg field goal, 24-14. Fred Cox ends the next drive with one for the Vikings, 24-17.

The Vikings hold the Skins on downs. On the first play from scrimmage Fran throws the bomb to Gilliam—46 yards. It's a touchdown! Fred Cox misses the extra point, 24-23.

The fourth quarter begins on the Viking 48-yard line. Brent McClanahan blasts up the middle 15 yards to the Redskin 37. The offensive line is starting to work on the Redskin defense and Brent gets six more yards on two carries to the Washington 31. Chuck Foreman slices through for six more to the 25. First and ten, the Redskin defense stiffens and two running plays lose six yards. On third down Fran hands off to Chuck.

He finds a bit of daylight in the middle of the Redskin line, and he's gone! Thirty-one yards down the middle. Washington 24, Vikings 30. But the game isn't over. Billy Kilmer, with 1:47 left, shocks the Vikings by going 77 yards for the winning touchdown. Final Score: Redskins 31, Vikings 30.

The game was lost, and it was the first loss of the season, but the people who watched the game saw a team that wouldn't give up. The man who is possibly the best example of Viking determination is Chuck Foreman. It is an attitude, which isn't so much spoken as it is shown. Chuck Foreman is the man who never gives up.

He was born Walter Eugene Foreman on October 26, 1950. He has been called Chuck almost since birth. The name was given to him by his mother. She was a fan of soap operas, and named him 'Chuck' after her favorite heroine's son. His name was Chuck. Somehow, it seems appropriate, for on the football field he is a very dramatic character.

He was the second of four children in a very dramatic family. His older brother, Francis, received a football scholarship to the University of Cincinnati. His younger brother, Gary, received a football scholarship from the University of Miami, and certainly Chuck was a football player.

Athletics was not the most important thing in the Foreman household. Education and development of character were very important. His sister went to Central State in Ohio on an academic scholarship and Chuck himself earned good grades at the University of Miami.

As a young boy, Chuck was sent to a Catholic grade school because his parents thought he would receive a good education there. During those years he had an experience which was to be very important. Chuck was a member of a playground recreational football team. He was obviously one of the better players on the team. But he wasn't playing very much. He was better in practice, and he was better in the games than the other backs. But he still didn't play much.

44

Finally in frustration, Chuck quit the team. A year passed, and football season arrived again. His coach asked him if he was going to go out for football again. Chuck told the coach that he didn't think so, but he would give it some thought. He talked to his father about his past frustrations, about how he felt that he had performed better than the other players and still hadn't become a starter. Mr. Foreman listened to Chuck. He thought about what Chuck had said and finally said, "You'll never play, unless you join the team. The only way to play is to go back and try harder." So, Chuck re-joined the team and eventually became a starter. "Never Give Up" was the lesson Chuck never forgot.

Chuck is very proud of his family, and looks back with pride to his early years. He refers to his family home as "the nicest house in the ghetto."

At Frederick High School his athletic ability became more obvious. He played football, basketball, and ran the hurdles for the track team. His speed and strength were most noticeable in track. By the time he graduated from high school he held the Maryland State high school record for the high hurdles (14.1) and the low hurdles (19.4).

Proving his talent in football was a little more difficult. In high school he played defensive tackle and tight end. He was good enough at defensive tackle to be recruited by the University of Miami. His speed quickly made Miami switch him to defensive secondary. He played cornerback his freshman year at Miami.

At a football practice session early in his second year, all the team was being timed for speed in the 40-yard dash. Surprisingly, the fastest man on the team was a cornerback, Chuck Foreman. Chuck soon became a running back.

After spending most of his sophomore year as a running back he became comfortable with the position. He was ready for his junior year.

It turned out to be a great year. Chuck rushed for 951 yards and 10 touchdowns—a school rushing record. The pro scouts were beginning to take notice, some even felt he might win the Heisman Trophy. His senior year was to be a season of great expectations

It didn't work out that way. Chuck did finish his last semester with a 3.2 grade point average. He earned his degree with a Bachelor of Arts in Education. But it was a different story on the football field.

Although he did gain 1555 yards rushing, receiving, and returning kicks, he did it as a wide receiver. Miami did not have a good year. Chuck had difficulty adjusting to the new position. The Heisman Trophy now was less likely to belong to Chuck since it usually went to a running back or a quarterback. Most of the pro scouts seemed to lose interest.

Foreman did have a good enough year to be invited to play in the post-season invitational games. He was awarded the Most Valuable Player Award for both the Senior Bowl and the North-South game.

A few scouts noticed that Chuck kept on trying, that he was versatile, that he was willing to learn. The scouts from Minnesota were so impressed that on January 30, 1973, Chuck Foreman was drafted by the Minnesota Vikings.

Since the arrival of Coach Bud Grant in 1967, the Vikings had won 53, lost 28, and tied three games. During that time they had won four Central Division Championships. Consequently, the 7-7 record in 1972 had the markings of a disaster. They finished third in a four-team division. The need for a running back was obvious. Minnesota fans wondered if Foreman could fill the gap.

His college coach at the University of Miami described

Chuck as "the greatest running back in the U.S., a super athlete who comes along only once in a coach's career." His new coach, Bud Grant, described him later "as the best of the three that we were considering in the draft because he is more versatile . . . . He is a man who can run inside or outside with speed."

Strangely the very qualities which had made his senior year seem unexciting to the pro scouts were the points of interest to the Vikings. The assets the Vikings were looking for were athletic character and versatility. Chuck had both, in quantity.

Versatility was the one quality the Vikings always looked for. They didn't look for the best receiver or the best passer, but the best athlete. They felt the quality would show regardless of the position. In the case of Chuck Foreman they were to be remarkably accurate.

Besides versatility, Chuck's character was attractive. A shy quiet young man, he seemed to have the temperament to fit well in the austere, disciplined machine of Bud Grant's Vikings.

The Viking training camp usually opens in late July. In 1973 the team started training with a purpose. They were determined to change that 7-7 record! But it wasn't going to be an easy job. The Vikings faced one of the toughest schedules that they had ever had:

Oakland, Green Bay (twice), San Francisco, and Cleveland. Five games against the previous year's playoff teams.

At the Vikings' training camp Chuck made steady progress. He broke into the Viking starting line-up in the second game of the season against the Chicago Bears. In 16 carries he gained 116 yards, caught four passes for 46 yards, and received the game ball from his teammates.

His quarterback, Fran Tarkenton, described Chuck after his first game, "The man is phenomenal. Nobody wants to put any extra burdens on his back by calling him the next great this or that. He has plenty to learn and he made some mistakes against the Bears. I'm talking about the natural ability he has.

"He does have Sayers' moves. And he's bigger. He's the kind of runner who when you get him through the line for five yards is going to get you 10 or 15 on his own. He runs, he catches the ball, he'll block and he's got the perfect temperament. He believes in himself, but he'll sacrifice for the team."

Foreman was the man the Vikings needed! Chuck went on to have a great year and the Vikings themselves had a great year only to lose in the Super Bowl to the Miami Dolphins.

At the annual Vikings Awards dinner Chuck was the unanimous choice for the best rookie, but that was only the beginning. He was selected as reserve running back for the Pro Bowl. He was the Associated Press' Offensive Rookie of the Year. He was voted the National Conference Rookie of the Year by the Hall of Fame Committee and received the Bert Bell Memorial Trophy.

In 1974, the Vikings again won the divisional title and went to the Super Bowl. Chuck also had a good year rushing for 777 yards. He was chosen at the Vikings Award dinner as the best offensive player. The Miami Touchdown Club named him Pro Football Player of the Year. Foreman was also chosen to be the starting running back in the Pro Bowl for the National conference, and was third in the voting for the Player of the Year Award.

By July, 1975, Chuck was ready to start his third season in the league. Soon everyone would know if he was another Gale Sayers, or just a flash in the pan. It was more difficult to be sure of his quality with the Vikings than it was with most teams. Bud Grant's coaching philosophy differs from most in that he tends to conserve the career of his backs.

If the game appears to be well in hand, the Vikings' starting running backs will probably be pulled from the game early. This aids greatly in extending the life of a running back. But it also tends to limit his chances to gain recognition. If a player doesn't play regularly, he can't gain 1,000 yards or score touchdowns.

The many awards that Chuck received during the post-season seemed to forecast good results for the coming year. The Vikings had been to the Super Bowl for the second straight year and were convinced that with Chuck Foreman they would be able to do the job again. The exhibition season started with losses to the New York Jets and the New England Patriots. Then the Vikings defeated the Miami Dolphins and the Dallas Cowboys.

Chuck didn't play much because the coaches were looking at the newcomers. The following week Chuck injured his knee during a scrimmage. He sat on the bench as the Vikings completed their exhibition season with a loss to the St. Louis Cardinals and an overtime tie with the lowly San Diego Chargers.

Finally the regular season opened on September 21st against the rebuilding San Francisco 49ers. Chuck did not start, but later in the game he carried the ball five times. One of those carries resulted in his first touchdown of the new season. The team won 27-17, and looked good doing it.

Foreman's knee was beginning to feel a lot better. Always cautious, Grant didn't start him although Chuck did get into the next game against Cleveland. He scored two touchdowns and the game turned into a rout as the Vikings won 42-10. His first touchdown was the conclusion of a forty-yard drive. The ball was on the one-yard line, Chuck took the handoff from quarterback Fran Tarkenton, crashed into the stiffened Browns line, then bounced to the left and leaned into the end zone.

As the Vikings prepared for their third game it became obvious that Chuck Foreman was now fully recovered. The Bears were their opponents, and despite the fact that Chicago had a lot of new faces, the Vikings knew their opponents would play ball like the Bears of old. They would be rough, aggressive, maybe a little more disciplined with their new coach, Jack Pardee, but still the ornery, chippy Bears. Chuck did start, gained 56 yards and scored one touchdown. His score was set up by a pass that was thrown to him, after he had slipped through the line, and broken to the inside. He caught it and steamed up the middle of the Bears' secondary to their two-yard line. He bolted over from the two on the next play. He didn't play much in the second half as the Vikings pulled away to win 28-3.

The following week the Vikings were to face the New York Jets. They owed the Jets one from the preseason and a huge crowd turned out to see the two great quarterbacks Francis Tarkenton and Joe Willie Namath duel each other. There were also two super running backs in the game, John Riggins of the Jets, who was to gain over 1,000 yards in spite of the pitiful Jets offensive line, and Chuck Foreman. The fans were not disappointed as the two teams played a very exciting game. Chuck had another good day. He carried the ball 25 times for 96 yards and scored three touchdowns.

Sportswriters started looking up NFL records for the most touchdowns scored in one year. They found 22 by the sensational Gale Sayers of the Chicago Bears. Chuck had now scored six in his first four games, and he hadn't even played much in the first two.

But, there wasn't really much time for him to be thinking about that achievement. The Vikings' main challengers for the Central Division title, the Detroit Lions, were next on the schedule.

The Lions, like the Bears, had a new coach. The Vikings and the Lions have played each other twice a year for the last seven years and the Lions have won only one game. Detroit was a team with a split personality under their new coach. They were organized, aggressive and disciplined when they were "in" a game, and given to cheap shots and late hits

when they were fading. They are also known for their surprises and trickiness. The Vikings used this characteristic to their advantage in the second quarter when Fran detected a double safety blitz. (This is a situation in which both deep defenders instead of covering their positions dash forward to make a tackle before the receivers can get out to catch a pass. One of the best moves to offset this is to send a big back up the middle.)

Fran saw this developing on the line of scrimmage and audibled a change. Fran called out the new signals, the ball was snapped, he handed off to Chuck. The right side of the Viking line grunted right and a hole opened. Chuck burst by the surprised Detroit linebacker and into the secondary for a 23-yard gain to the Lion four-yard line. On the next play Fran passed to the tight end Stu Voight for the touchdown. The Vikings won 25-19. Chuck gained 107 yards on the ground. It was his first 100-yard day of the year. He seemed to have recovered from the injured knee.

In their sixth game the Vikings went to Chicago to play the Bears again. It was a crucial game for the Vikings, for they had to maintain their lead over the Lions in the division. The Bears threw a scare into the Vikings, scrapping with them the whole game only to lose 13-9. Chuck Foreman enjoyed another 100 yard day, carrying the ball 25 times for 102 yards.

The Vikings were now in a comfortable position to gain the title again, provided they continued their level of play. The Packers were the Vikings' next opponent. Green Bay had its own premiere running back — the quick starting, bull-like John Brockington. On the first play from scrimmage Brockington carried the ball and was hit so hard that his thigh pad was completely reversed in his pants and he had to leave the game with a severely bruised thigh. He never returned. It was that kind of a game, and the lead see-sawed back and forth till the fourth quarter, when the Vikings' conditioning began to make a difference.

Minnesota used an old, reliable play. Fran Tarkenton isolated his fast, 215-pound running back on a slower 220-pound linebacker. There was no contest. Fran threw as Chuck broke to the outside and pulled the right side linebacker with him. Chuck went 32 yards to the Green Bay 14. A touchdown soon followed. The final score was Vikings 28, Green Bay 17.

As the season reached the halfway point Foreman had gained 474 yards rushing, caught 34 passes and scored 8 touchdowns. Probably the most important fact is that of the 474 yards gained, 377 had been gained in the last four games.

The next game was a rout. The Atlanta Falcons were outclassed as Chuck scored three touchdowns in the first half.

49
10

The following week against New Orleans, the Viking defensive team duplicated the job that they did on the Falcons; total net offense 60 yards. As his offensive line blew the disorganized Saints off the ball, Chuck rushed for 117 yards and caught 6 passes.

The Vikings were marching through the easy part of their schedule which concluded against the San Diego Chargers. Chuck had his best day of the year. Playing again only a little more than half the game he gained 127 yards and scored three touchdowns. The Vikings were now 10-0-0, and very close to another division title. Four days later the Los Angeles Rams gave them the title, beating the Lions on Thanksgiving Day, 20-0. It was Minnesota's seventh Central Division title in eight years.

The rest of the season seemed less important now as the title was wrapped up and Minnesota had to prepare for the playoff. They played the exciting game against the Redskins, their first loss, bounced back against the Packers, a 24-3 rout. They lost their second game to the Detroit Lions at Pontiac, Michigan. There Chuck and the Vikings had their poorest day of the year. It was revenge for the Lions who had left Bloomington earlier in the year soundly beaten and had vowed that they would whip the Vikings in their second match. They meant it. According to Bud Grant, "it was a fanny-kicking contest and Detroit brought the shoe." The Lions won 17-10.

This left the Buffalo Bills. They had a poor defense, but as everyone knew with O. J. Simpson they didn't always need a defense. The game had been built up as a confrontation of the two best ground gainers of each conference and was well attended despite a heavy snow that fell throughout the game.

The Vikings had a reason for wanting to win; they wanted some momentum to take into the playoffs. They scored the first two times that they had the ball. Chuck himself had a little extra motivation as he scored the first touchdown, breaking two tackles as he ran the ball in from the four-yard line. In the second quarter he slammed into linebacker Doug Allen, spun to his left and walked into the end zone for his second touchdown of the day. He scored his third touchdown on a little swing pass from Fran, which was the pass that enabled Tarkenton to tie the great John Unitas for the most career touchdown passes.

Towards the end of the game a recovered fumble gave the Vikings the ball on the Bill's 38-yard line. Six plays later Fran threw a second touchdown pass to Chuck to break John Unitas' record, and to tie Chuck with Gayle Sayers and O. J. Simpson for the most touchdowns in a season. Quite a day for the record keepers! But that wasn't all, for 24 seconds later reserve quarterback Gary Marangi of the Bills threw to a streaking O. J. for a 64-yard touchdown play to put Simpson into the record books all by himself. The game ended with the Vikings winning, 35-13. In the individual competition O.J. scored two touchdowns, carried for 57 yards and caught three passes for 66 yards. Chuck scored four touchdowns, carried for 85 yards and caught ten passes for 87 yards.

Foreman's rushing total for the year was 1070 yards. He caught 73 passes, and scored 22 touchdowns. But for six more yards gained by Jim Otis of the Cardinals, Chuck would have won the triple crown of yardage, receptions, and touchdowns scored for the National Football Conference, something no other back has ever done.

The Vikings lost the first game of the playoffs to the Dallas Cowboys, 17-14. Once again they were stopped short of a Super Bowl win. But the real significance of the 1975 season could not be overlooked. Chuck Foreman had become the Vikings' star running back. And even more important, his youth and determination made him one of the most promising running backs in modern football history.

Football
Johnny Unitas
Bob Griese
Vince Lombardi
Joe Namath
O. J. Simpson
Fran Tarkenton
Roger Staubach
Alan Page
Larry Csonka
Don Shula
Franco Harris
Terry Bradshaw
Chuck Foreman

Baseball
Frank Robinson
Tom Seaver
Jackie Robinson
Johnny Bench
Hank Aaron
Roberto Clemente
Mickey Mantle
Rod Carew
Fred Lynn
Pete Rose

Basketball
Walt Frazier
Kareem Abdul Jabbar
Wilt Chamberlain
Jerry West
Bill Russell
Bill Walton
Bob McAdoo
Julius Erving
John Havlicek
Rick Barry
George McGinnis

superstars!
superstars!
superstars!

CREATIVE EDUCATION SPORTS SUPERSTARS

Tennis
Jimmy Connors
Chris Evert
Pancho Gonzales
Evonne Goolagong
Arthur Ashe
Billie Jean King
Stan Smith

Racing
Peter Revson
Jackie Stewart
A. J. Foyt
Richard Petty

Miscellaneous
Mark Spitz
Muhammad Ali
Secretariat
Olga Korbut
Evel Knievel
Jean Claude Killy
Janet Lynn
Peggy Fleming
Pelé
Rosi Mittermaier
Sheila Young
Dorothy Hamill
Nadia Comaneci

Golf
Lee Trevino
Jack Nicklaus
Arnold Palmer
Johnny Miller
Kathy Whitworth
Laura Baugh

Hockey
Phil and Tony Esposito
Gordie Howe
Bobby Hull
Bobby Orr